Vol
Pieces, Parts, & Percentages

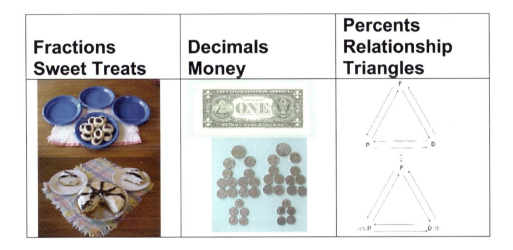

Fractions Sweet Treats	Decimals Money	Percents Relationship Triangles

© 2012 Jean Marie Miscisin, MLS, MA

**Pieces, Parts, and Percentages
Fractions, Decimals, and Percents**

© 2012 Jean Marie Miscisin, MLS, MA

All rights reserved.

ISBN: 10: 1477621733
ISBN: 13: 9781477621738

INTRODUCTION

Pieces, Parts, and Percentages - is Volume 3 in the **4-COLOR LESSONS** Series. This book is divided into two major sections.

In the first section, Concepts needed to understand Mathematical relationships are introduced; Fractions with Sweet Treats, Decimal-Fractions with Money, and Percents with Relationship Triangles.

In the second section, Twenty Strengths and Twelve Preferences for the Learning Environment are listed for each of the **4-COLOR STYLES.**

Design each lesson using four or more of the strengths from each **COLOR STYLE**.

Set the goal to strengthen ALL **4-COLOR STYLES** in every learner.

These fun activities and open ended questions provide ways to increase student comprehension of these complex Mathematical concepts.

This book is ideal for individual and small group instruction - Tutorial and Home School settings.

Fractions - Sweet Treats

Fractions - Sweet Treats

All fractions have a NUMERATOR and a DENOMINATOR.

The NUMERATOR represents the PARTS or PIECES in the FRACTION.

The NUMERATOR is the DIVIDEND in calculating solutions to problems.

NUMERATOR = DIVIDEND = a number or quantity to be divided by another number.

The DENOMINATOR represents the WHOLE and its relation to its parts.

The DENOMINATOR is the DIVISOR in calculating solutions to problems.

DENOMINATOR = DIVISOR = a number or quantity by which another number is divided.

FRACTIONS are read from top NUMERATOR down to the DENOMINATOR:

One Half = 1/2 = 1 ÷ 2 =
One = NUMERATOR = DIVIDEND
Two = DENOMINATOR = DIVISOR

Two Sevenths = 2/7 = 2 ÷ 7 =
Two = NUMERATOR = DIVIDEND
Seven = DENOMINATOR = DIVISOR

Three Fourths = 3/4 = 3 ÷ 4 =
Three = NUMERATOR = DIVIDEND
Four = DENOMINATOR = DIVISOR

The concept of "one whole" in FRACTIONS:

FRACTIONS are read from top NUMERATOR down to the DENOMINATOR:

One divided by one – when one whole item is displayed.

Eight divided by eight – when one whole item is still present but divided into eight parts. I used melted chocolate on a Lemon Meringue Pie to designate the eight pieces of pie.

	1/1	One whole pie One divided by one = one $1 \div 1 = 1$
	8/8	Eight eighths of one pie Eight divided by eight = one $8 \div 8 = 1$

	6/6	Six sixths of one Cherry pie

Six divided by six = one
6 ÷ 6 = 1 |
| | 2/2 | Two halves of one pan of brownies
Two divided by two = one whole pan of brownies
2 ÷ 2 = 1 |
| | 12/12 | One plate with one dozen cookies
Twelve divided by twelve = one plate of cookies
12 ÷ 12 = 1 |
| | 24/24 | Two plates with one dozen cookies on each = one set
Twenty four divided by twenty four = one set of 24.
24 ÷ 24 = 1 |

	8/8	Eight eighths of one pie Eight divided by eight = one 8 ÷ 8 = 1
	8/8 − 2/8 = 6/8	Eight eighths minus two eighths equals six eighths.

8/8 − 2/8 = 6/8
Eight eighths minus two eighths equals six eighths.

Reduce to lower terms:
When both the Numerator and the Denominator can be evenly divided by the same number, the FRACTION can be reduced to lowest terms.

2/8 can be divided evenly by 2 = 1/4 one fourth.
Two divided by two equals one.
Eight divided by two equals four.
Two eighths of the pie equals one fourth of the pie.

6/8 can be divided evenly by 2 = 3/4 three fourths.
Six divided by two equals three.
Eight divided by two equals four.
Six eighths of the pie equals three fourths of the pie.

	6/6	Six sixths of one Cherry pie Six divided by six = one 6 ÷ 6 = 1
	6/6 − 2/6 = 4/6	Six sixths minus two sixths equals four sixths.

6/6 − 2/6 = 4/6
Six sixths minus two sixths equals four sixths.

Reduce to lower terms:
When both the Numerator and the Denominator can be evenly divided by the same number, the FRACTION can be reduced to lowest terms.

2/6 can be divided evenly by 2 = 1/3 one third.
Two divided by two equals one.
Six divided by two equals three.
Two sixths of Cherry pie equals one third of the pie.

4/6 can be divided evenly by 2 = 2/3 two thirds.
4 divided by two equals two.
Six divided by two equals three.
Four sixths of Cherry pie equals two thirds of the pie.

	1/2 + 2/4 = 4/4 = 1 pan of Brownies	Draw one line to cut the 1/2 into the same size pieces, Then you can see the 4/4 in the pan.
	3/3 + 2/4 = 12/12 = 1 pan of Brownies	Draw one line horizontally on left 1/2 = 6/12 of Pan. Draw two lines Vertically on right 2/4 = 6/12 6/12 + 6/12 = 12/12 = 1 Full pan
	12/ 12 = 1 Plate of one dozen cookies	Twelve cookies equals one whole plate of cookies 12 ÷ 12 = 1
	1/3 of 12/1 = 4 Cookies on each plate.	**1/3 X 12/1 = 12/3 = 4 Cookies 4/12 = Reduce to lower terms - divide both by 4 = 1/3 on each plate.**

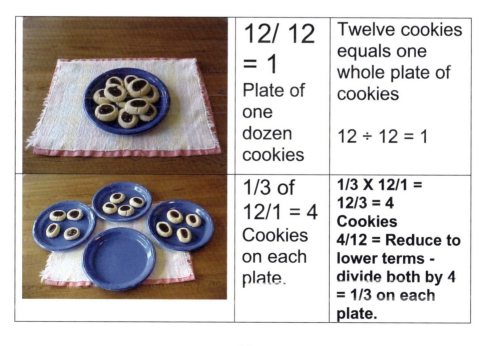

Reducing Fractions to Lowest Terms = 1/2
General Rule = Lowest Terms Means Larger Pieces
Divide both Numerator and Denominator by the same number.

2/4 = 1/2 One Step ÷ 2	$\dfrac{2}{4} = \dfrac{2 \div 2}{4 \div 2} = \dfrac{1}{2}$
3/6 = 1/2 One Step ÷ 3	$\dfrac{3}{6} = \dfrac{3 \div 3}{6 \div 3} = \dfrac{1}{2}$
4/8 = 1/2 One Step ÷ 4	$\dfrac{4}{8} = \dfrac{4 \div 4}{8 \div 4} = \dfrac{1}{2}$
4/8 = 1/2 Step One ÷ 2 Step Two ÷ 2	$\dfrac{4}{8} = \dfrac{4 \div 2}{8 \div 2} = \dfrac{2}{4}$ $\dfrac{2}{4} = \dfrac{2 \div 2}{4 \div 2} = \dfrac{1}{2}$
6/12 = 1/2 One Step ÷ 6	$\dfrac{6}{12} = \dfrac{6 \div 6}{12 \div 6} = \dfrac{1}{2}$
6/12 = 1/2 Step One ÷ 3 Step Two ÷ 2	$\dfrac{6}{12} = \dfrac{6 \div 3}{12 \div 3} = \dfrac{2}{4}$ $\dfrac{2}{4} = \dfrac{2 \div 2}{4 \div 2} = \dfrac{1}{2}$
12/24 = 1/2 One Step ÷ 12	$\dfrac{12}{24} = \dfrac{12 \div 12}{24 \div 12} = \dfrac{1}{2}$

12/24 = 1/2 Step One ÷ 2 Step Two ÷ 3 Step Three ÷ 2	$\dfrac{12}{24} = \dfrac{12 \div 2}{24 \div 2} = \dfrac{6}{12}$ $\dfrac{6}{12} = \dfrac{6 \div 3}{12 \div 3} = \dfrac{2}{4}$ $\dfrac{2}{4} = \dfrac{2 \div 2}{4 \div 2} = \dfrac{1}{2}$
12/24 = 1/2 Step One ÷ 3 Step Two ÷ 2 Step Three ÷ 2	$\dfrac{12}{24} = \dfrac{12 \div 3}{24 \div 3} = \dfrac{4}{8}$ $\dfrac{4}{8} = \dfrac{4 \div 2}{8 \div 2} = \dfrac{2}{4}$ $\dfrac{2}{4} = \dfrac{2 \div 2}{4 \div 2} = \dfrac{1}{2}$
12/24 = 1/2 Step One ÷ 4 Step Two ÷ 3	$\dfrac{12}{24} = \dfrac{12 \div 4}{24 \div 4} = \dfrac{3}{6}$ $\dfrac{3}{6} = \dfrac{3 \div 3}{6 \div 3} = \dfrac{1}{2}$

Some of the Fractions presented in this section will be converted to Decimals in the following section.

Reducing Fractions to Lowest Terms
General Rule = Lowest Terms Means Larger Pieces
These Fractions cannot be reduced to 1/2 by dividing both Numerator and Denominator by the same number.
OR The fraction cannot be reduced by dividing both the Numerator and Denominator by the same number.

2/6 = 1/3 One Step ÷ 2	$\underline{2} = \underline{2 \div 2} = \underline{1}$ $6 = 6 \div 2 = 3$
4/6 = 2/3 One Step ÷ 2	$\underline{4} = \underline{4 \div 2} = \underline{2}$ $6 = 6 \div 2 = 3$
2/7 = 2/7	Cannot be reduced
5/9 = 5/9	Cannot be reduced

These fractions cannot be converted to even-decimals. They always end up with a Remainder Fraction.

1 ÷ 3 = 0.33333 with the Remainder 1/3

$$3\overline{)1}$$
One divided by three.

$$3\overline{)1.00}$$
One divided by three.
Place decimal in answer.

```
  0. 3
3 )1.00
  09
```
Three times three equals nine.

```
  0. 33
3 )1.00
  09
   10
   09
    1/3
```
Since One is always the remainder the answer will never come out evenly.

Decimals - Money

Decimal-Fractions
Yes, Decimals are another way of writing Fractions

Money - $1.00

Money is a medium of exchange for "real" goods.
For this book one dollar will be used to represent "one whole" –
Since there are 100 – one hundred cents in one dollar, the transition to percentages is easier than from fractions.

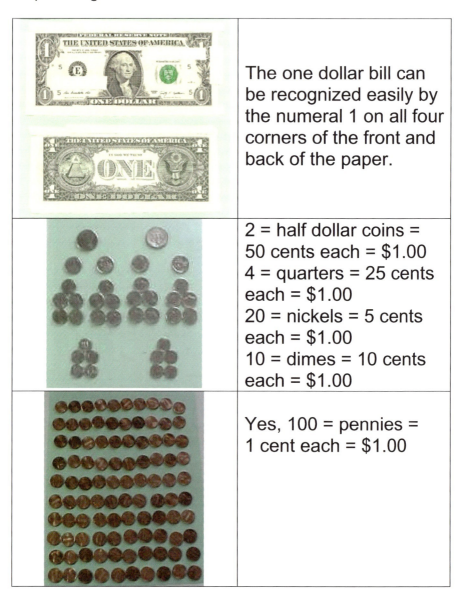

	The one dollar bill can be recognized easily by the numeral 1 on all four corners of the front and back of the paper.
	2 = half dollar coins = 50 cents each = $1.00
4 = quarters = 25 cents each = $1.00
20 = nickels = 5 cents each = $1.00
10 = dimes = 10 cents each = $1.00
	Yes, 100 = pennies = 1 cent each = $1.00

Money - $1.00 = 100 cents

One Coin = Fraction of $1.00
One hundred pennies = One hundred cents

1 half dollar coin = 50 cents	How many in $1.00 = 2 How many do you see = 1 Numerator = 1 Denominator = 2 **1/2 of 100 pennies = 50 cents** 1/2 of 1.00 = .50 1/2 X 1.00 = .50 1 ÷ 2 = 0.50
1 quarter coin = 25 cents	How many in $1.00 = 4 How many do you see = 1 Numerator = 1 Denominator = 4 **1/4 of 100 pennies = 25 cents** 1/4 of 1.00 = .25 1/4 X 1.00 = .25 1 ÷ 4 = 0.25
1 dime coin = 10 cents	How many in $1.00 = 10 How many do you see = 1 Numerator = 1 Denominator = 10 **1/10 of 100 pennies= 10cents** 1/10 of 1.00 = .10 1/10 X 1.00 = .10 1 ÷ 10 = 0.10
1 nickel coin = 5 cents	How many in $1.00 = 20 How many do you see = 1 Numerator = 1 Denominator = 20 **1/20 of 100 pennies= 5cents** 1/20 of 1.00 = .05 1/20 X 1.00 = .05 1 ÷ 20 = 0.05

Important terms used in converting Fractions to Decimal Equivalents

Original whole number = Denominator = Divisor
Parts or pieces = Numerator = Dividend
Answer = Quotient

$\underline{3}$ = Parts or pieces = Numerator = Dividend
4 = Original whole number = Denominator = Divisor

3 ÷ 4 =

3 = Parts or pieces = Numerator = Dividend
÷ = Divided by
4 = Original whole number = Denominator = Divisor

$$4\overline{)3}$$

Yes, in this format the Numerator = Dividend is placed inside the Division Sign and the Denominator = Divisor is placed outside the bracket.

Numbers that come BEFORE the DECIMAL POINT are always WHOLE NUMBERS.

Behind every whole number is a decimal point.
This fact is "understood" when the numeral is a whole number.

Numbers that come AFTER the DECIMAL POINT are always PARTS or PIECES.

The DECIMAL POINT must be placed behind the whole number in the DIVIDEND before calculating the QUOTIENT.

The DECIMAL POINT must be placed in the QUOTIENT directly ABOVE the DECIMAL POINT in the DIVIDEND.

What? "of" means multiply in Fractions

1/2 of 1.00 = .50

1/2 X 1.00 = .50 $\frac{1}{2}$ X $\frac{1.00}{1}$ = $\frac{1.00}{2}$

1.00 ÷ 2 = 0.50   and   1 ÷ 2 = 0.50

```
  ___
2)1
```
One divided by two.
One is a whole number.
Place a decimal point behind one.

```
   .__
2)1.00
```
One dollar divided by two.
Place decimal in Quotient.

```
  0. 5
2)1.0
  10
```
Five times two equals ten.

```
  0. 50
2)1.00
  10
  00
```
Since one-hundred cents equals one dollar, add the zero to equal fifty cents.

One half of one dollar equals fifty cents.

1/4 of 1.00 = .25

1/4 X 1.00 = .25 $\frac{1}{4}$ X $\frac{1.00}{1}$ = $\frac{1.00}{4}$

1.00 ÷ 4 = 0.25   and   1 ÷ 4 = 0.25

$\overline{}$
4)1   One divided by four.

$\overline{^{\,.}}$
4)1.00   One dollar divided by four.
                                        Place decimal in Quotient.

$\underline{0.\,2}$
4)1.0   Two times four equals eight.
$\underline{08}$ Remainder 2.
2

$\underline{0.\,25}$
4)1.00   Since one-hundred cents equals
$\underline{08}$ one dollar, add the zero and bring
20 the zero down and divide by four
$\underline{20}$ again, five times four equals twenty.

One fourth of one dollar equals twenty-five cents.

1/10 of 1.00 = .10

1/10 X 1.00 = .10 $\dfrac{1}{10}$ X $\dfrac{1.00}{1}$ = $\dfrac{1.00}{10}$

1.00 ÷ 2 = 0.50   and   1 ÷ 2 = 0.50

$10\overline{)1}$ One divided by ten.

$10\overline{)1.00}$ (decimal placed in quotient) One dollar divided by ten. Place decimal in Quotient.

$\begin{array}{r}0.\,1\\10\overline{)1.0}\\\underline{10}\end{array}$ One times ten equals ten.

$\begin{array}{r}0.\,10\\10\overline{)1.00}\\\underline{10}\\00\end{array}$ Since one-hundred cents equals one dollar, add the zero to equal ten cents.

One tenth of one dollar equals ten cents.

1/20 of 1.00 = .05

1/20 X 1.00 = .05 $\dfrac{1}{20}$ X $\dfrac{1.00}{1}$ = $\dfrac{1.00}{20}$

1.00 ÷ 20 = 0.05 and   1 ÷ 20 = 0.05

$20\overline{)1}$ One divided by twenty.

$20\overline{)1.00}$ (with decimal point marked)   One dollar divided by twenty.
Place decimal in Quotient.

```
   0. 0
20 )1.0
      0
```
Ten cannot be divided by twenty, use Zero as a place holder in the answer.

```
   0. 05
20 )1.00
     00
    100
    100
```
Since one-hundred cents equals one dollar, add the zero and bring down one hundred and divide by twenty. Five times twenty equals one hundred.

One twentieth of one dollar equals five cents.

Two Coins = Fraction of $1.00
One hundred pennies = One hundred cents

2 half dollar coins = $1.00	How many in $1.00 = 2 How many do you see = 2 Numerator = 2 Denominator = 2 2/2 of 1.00 = 1.00 2/2 X 1.00 = 1.00 2 ÷ 2 = 1.00
2 quarter coins = 50 cents	How many in $1.00 = 4 How many do you see = 2 Numerator = 2 Denominator = 4 **2/4 of 100 pennies = 50 cents** 2/4 of 1.00 = .50 2/4 X 1.00 = .50 2 ÷ 4 = 0.50
2 dime coins = 20 cents	How many in $1.00 = 10 How many do you see = 2 Numerator = 2 Denominator = 10 **2/10 of 100 pennies = 20 cents** 2/10 of 1.00 = .20 2/10 X 1.00 = .20 2 ÷ 10 = 0.20
2 nickel coins = 10 cents	How many in $1.00 = 20 How many do you see = 2 Numerator = 2 Denominator = 20 **2/20 of 100 pennies= 10 cents** 2/20 of 1.00 = .10 2/20 X 1.00 = .10 2 ÷ 20 = 0.05

Percents - Relationship Triangles

F

P   **D**

$\frac{3}{4}$

F

75% **P**   **D** .75

Computing Parts-to-whole Relationships

Once you understand how to express a parts-to-whole relationship in fractions, then you can learn how to express the same fractions as decimal-fractions, and then percents. There are some steps you can take to calculate the equivalent relationships between fractions, decimal-fractions, and percents. Listed are some questions to assist the learner to think through the step-by-step processes needed to:

CHANGE a Fraction to a Decimal-Fraction

CHANGE a Decimal-Fraction to a Fraction

CHANGE a Fraction to a Percent

CHANGE a Decimal-Fraction to a Percent

CHANGE a Percent to a Fraction

CHANGE a Percent to a Decimal-Fraction

These operations graphically portrayed using 3/4, .75, 75%. See this Relationship Triangle Graphic Organizer on the next page.

On the pages following the Relationship Triangle Graphic Organizer there are questions to ask while thinking through the relationships between fractions, decimal-fractions, and percents in order to calculate the equivalent statements of the parts-to-whole relationships.

How to use the Relationships Triangles

1. Using the sample RELATIONSHIP TRIANGLES for 3/4, 1/2, and 1/4, start with the fraction and follow the downward arrow to the decimal-fraction.
2. Follow the directions to **CHANGE a Fraction to a Decimal-Fraction.**
3. Using the sample RELATIONSHIP TRIANGLES start with the decimal-fraction and follow the upward arrow to the fraction.
4. Follow the directions to **CHANGE a Decimal - Fraction to a Fraction.**
5. In order to solve problems with percents, you must first change the percent to either a decimal-fraction or fraction. Use the directions on the following pages.

Relationship Triangles

This Relationship Triangle Graphic Organizer uses ARROWS TO PORTRAY the six operations used to calculate the parts-to-whole relationships of **3/4, .75, 75%**.

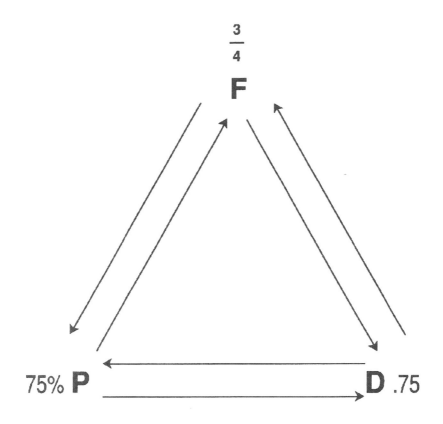

CHANGE a Fraction to a Decimal-Fraction

Questions to ask when starting with a FRACTION:

1. How many pieces were in the original whole number?

2. How many parts are in this parts-to-whole relationship?

3. How is this fraction read?
    Example: 3/4 = three fourths

4. How is this fraction read as an operational statement to change this fraction to a decimal-fraction statement?
    Answer: Three divided by four.

5. How can this fraction be rewritten to show this operation?
    Example: $\dfrac{3}{4}$ = 3 ÷ 4 = $\dfrac{}{4\,)\,3}$

6. After rewriting the fraction as an operational statement, what is needed before starting to calculate the answer?
    Answer: Behind every whole number there is a decimal point.

7. What should be done with decimal points in converting the fraction to a decimal-fraction?
    Answer: Place a decimal point behind the Dividend and place a decimal point in the quotient, directly above the decimal point in the dividend.

8. Since the divisor is a whole number does it need a decimal point?
    Answer: Since the divisor must be a whole number, leave the divisor as is.

9. How many places behind the decimal point should the quotient be calculated?
    Answer: Unless a story problem directs otherwise, zeros can be added to the Dividend until the answer, quotient, ends evenly without a remainder or until there is a repetition of a number or a series of same numbers or a pattern of numbers.

10. What do I do, if there is a repetition of a number or numbers?

Answer: if the last number is five (5) or higher ROUND UP to the next number. If the number is lower than five (5), ROUND OFF. In other words drop the next number.

11. What is the decimal-fraction equivalent of this fraction?
    Example: 3/4 = .75 or 0.75

12. What should be done to change a fraction to a percent?
    Answer: First change the fraction to a decimal-fraction then follow the steps to change a decimal-fraction to a percent.

3/4

$$4\overline{)3}$$ Three divided by four.

$$4\overline{)3.0}$$ Three divided by four.
     Place decimal in Quotient.

```
  0. 7
4 )3.0
  28
   2
```
Seven times four equals twenty-eight.
Remainder 2.

```
  0. 75
4 )3.00
  28
   20
   20
```
Add another zero and bring the zero down and divide by four again, five times four equals twenty.

The decimal-fraction equivalent of the Fraction 3/4 Three-fourths is 0.75.

CHANGE a Decimal - Fraction to a Fraction

Questions to ask when starting with a DECIMAL – FRACTION:

1. What is the place value of the decimal-fraction?
   Example: .75 is carried to the hundredths place.

2. How should this decimal-fraction read?
   Example: .75 = seventy-five hundredths

3. How would this decimal-fraction be read as an operational statement in order to change this decimal-fraction to a fraction?
   Example:

   .75 = seventy-five divided by one hundred
   $$= \frac{75}{100} = \frac{\text{seventy-five}}{\text{divided by}}\ \text{one hundred}$$

4. How can this fraction be reduced to lowest terms?
   Answer: Find a number by which both the numerator and denominator can be divided evenly.

   Example: $\dfrac{75 \div 5}{100 \div 5} = \dfrac{15 \div 5}{20 \div 5} = \dfrac{3}{4}$

   $\dfrac{3}{4} = \dfrac{75 \div 25}{100 \div 25} = \dfrac{3}{4}$

STEPS TO CHANGE a Fraction to a Percent

1. Change the FRACTION to a DECIMAL-FRACTION.
2. Change the decimal-fraction to a percentage

STEPS TO CHANGE a Decimal - Fraction to a Percentage

1. What can be done to change this decimal-fraction to a percentage statement?
   Answer: Since the percent sign means divided by one hundred, use the inverse operation of division which is multiplication and multiply the decimal-fraction by one hundred.

   Example: .75 X 100 =

   .75   First step to relocate
   X 100   the decimal point
   7500   behind the 5.

2. What do I have to remember about all whole numbers?
   Behind every whole number there is a "decimal point.

3. What should I do next?
   Count back from the last digit in the whole number, the same number of digits that are behind the decimal point in the number representing the parts in this relationship; drop the zeros, and add the percent sign.

   Example: 75%   Last step to change a
                       Decimal-Fraction to a
                       Percentage.

STEPS TO CHANGE a Percent to a Fraction

Questions to Ask Yourself When You Start with a Percentage

1. How could I rewrite this percentage relationship in words?
   Example: 75% = seventy-five percent

2. Since the percent sign means divided by one hundred, what is the parts number that is divided by one hundred?
   Example: 75 = seventy-five parts of the one hundred percent whole.

3. How could I rewrite the words as a fraction statement without reducing to lowest terms?

$$\frac{75}{100}$$

4. Now, how could I change this percentage to a fraction?

Example: $\dfrac{75 \div 5}{100 \div 5} = \dfrac{15 \div 5}{20 \div 5} = \dfrac{3}{4}$

$$\frac{75 \div 25}{100 \div 25} = \frac{3}{4}$$

STEPS TO CHANGE a Percent to a Decimal - Fraction

Questions to Ask Yourself When You Start with a Percentage

1. How can I rewrite this percentage to an operational statement to figure out the decimal-fraction equivalent?

   Example: 75%   75 ÷ 100 =

2. After rewriting the percentage as an operation statement what do I have to remember?
   Behind every whole number there is a "decimal point.

3. What do I do with the decimal point in the dividend?
   Place the decimal point behind the five.

4. What do I do with the decimal point in the Quotient?
   Place the decimal point above the decimal point in the dividend.

```
      . 
     ___
100 )75.0
```
   Seventy-five divided by one hundred.

5. How many places should I carry out my answer?
   because the hundredths place is two places behind the decimal point and the number is being divided by one hundred two zeros should be placed behind the decimal point

```
      . 
     ___
100 )75.00
```
   Seventy-five divided by one hundred.

6. What is the decimal-fraction equivalent of this percentage?

```
     0 .75
    _____
100 )75.00
     700
     ___
     500
     500
     ___
```

Seventy-five hundredths =
0.75 = .75

7. What do I do if there is a repetition of a number or the same series of numbers?

    If there is a repetition of the same number =
Example: 3333
This percentage will be more easily figured using a fraction statement.
= 1/3   This number cannot be divided evenly without a remainder.

    If there are a series of numbers that repeat =
Example: 142857 142857
This percentage will be more easily figured using a fraction statement.
= 1/7   This number cannot be divided evenly without a remainder.

*******   *******   *******   *******

Fractions for Applications

These fractions are more challenging and are to be used with the strengths and preferences in **4-COLOR LESSONS**.

The parts-to-whole relationships for the following fractions are presented at the end of this book.

$$\frac{5}{8} \quad \frac{1}{3} \quad \frac{5}{6} \quad \frac{1}{6} \quad \frac{7}{9} \quad \frac{1}{7}$$

Follow the steps in this book and see if you can arrive at the same solutions.

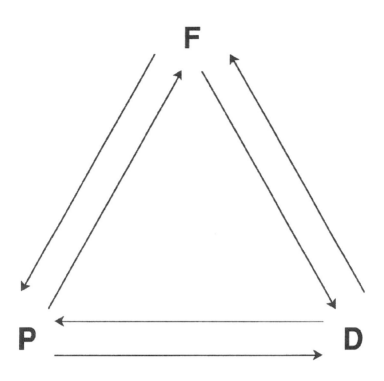

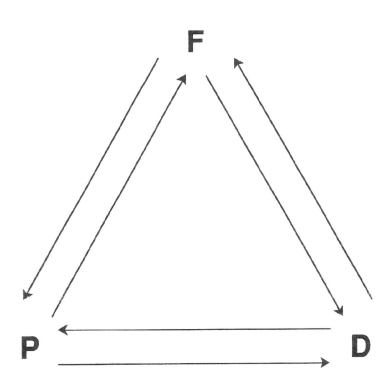

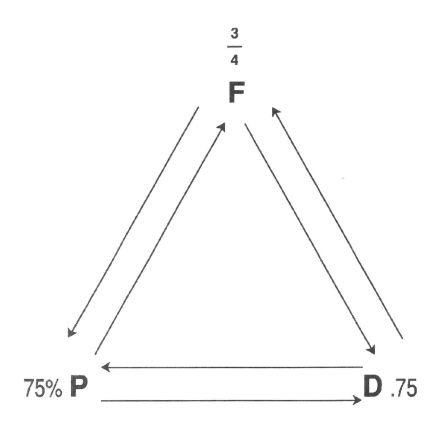

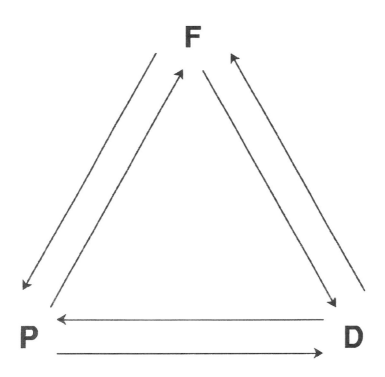

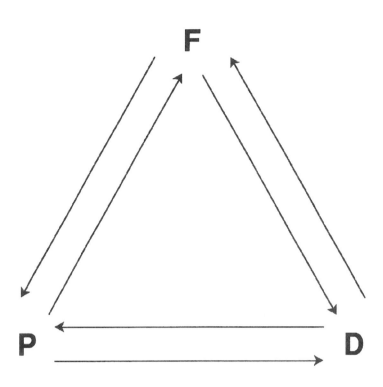

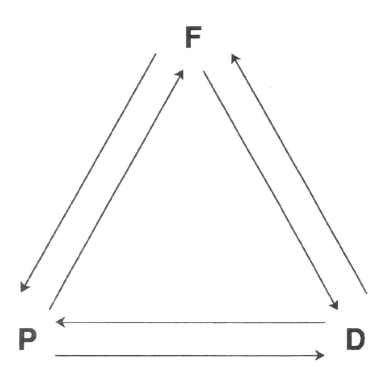

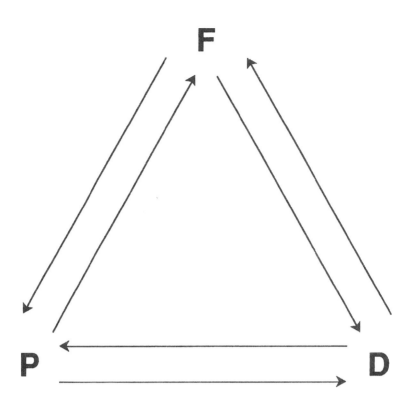

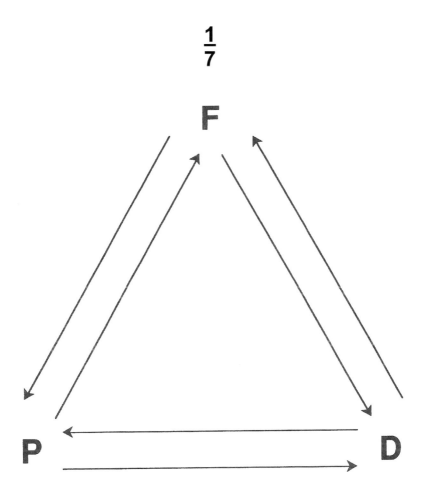

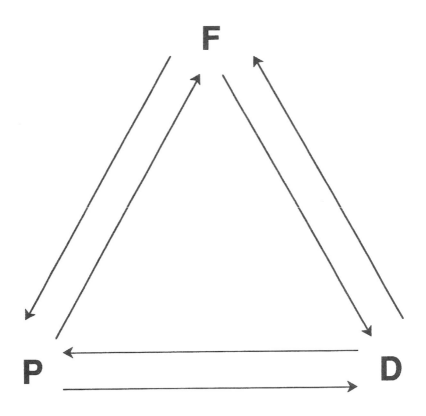

This Relationship Triangle can be used for the Fraction 1/6

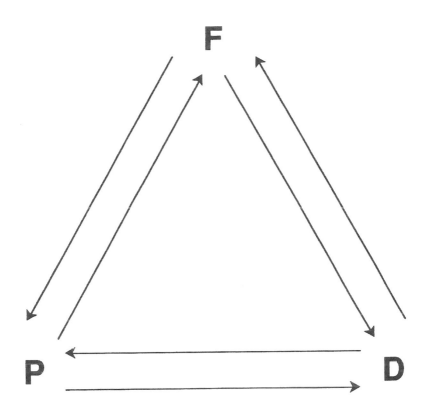

© 2012 Jean Marie Miscisin, MLS, MA

Copies of this Relationship Triangle may be made by the person using this book as long as the copyright is included.

4 QUICK TIPS

BLUE
Add Discussion time
Partner Activities
Discuss Feelings
Request Creative Responses

GOLD
Add Student Responsibility
Use Graphic Organizers
Provide Written Guidelines
Opportunities for practice

GREEN
Add Thinking Time
Allow Questions
Student Inventions
Research Opportunities

ORANGE
Add Movement
Game-Like Activity
Hands-On Projects
Improvisational Drama

*******   *******   *******   *******

THIS PREFERENCE ORDER INCREASES COMPREHENSION
WHEN WORKING WITH INDIVIDUAL STUDENTS

ORANGE = Kinesthetic, Tactile, Visual, Auditory

GREEN = Tactile, Visual, Auditory, Kinesthetic

BLUE = Auditory, Visual, Tactile, Kinesthetic

GOLD = Visual, Auditory, Tactile, Kinesthetic

*******   *******   *******   *******

ORANGE Strengths:

Take charge orientation	Keep options open
Being the master of tools	Negotiating
Free spirited	Make an impact
Thriving during chaos	Spotting/seizing opportunities
Determination	Risk-taking
Direct communicators	Trouble-shooting
Doing many things at once	Exceed limitations
Changing	Welcoming adventure
Adaptability	Thinking on the spot
Action	Expediency

Copyright 2006 by Mary Miscisin – All rights reserved
www.PositivelyMary.com
Used with permission.

ORANGE Preferences in the Learning Environment

Included in a lesson I would like Competition.

I enjoy a lesson more when it includes Games.

I need opportunities for making Choices.

In a lesson I prefer Variety with practical practice.

I take in information through all my Senses.

Lessons can be supported by Improvisation.

I am a Dynamic Learner.

I am frequently Spontaneous.

I prefer Game-like Skill-building.

I want my lessons to be Active.

I appreciate Cleverness.

I strive for impact.

ORANGE – STUDENT BEHAVIOR SAMPLES

ORANGE - LINGO
- Let's play a game.
- When do we get to do something?
- I'll bet I can say these words faster?
- That takes too long.

ORANGE – BODY LANGUAGE
- Wiggles in the chair.
- Takes the "LONG" way to a chair or table.
- Draws or "doodles" while listening.
- Grabs the crayons or pencils and starts passing them around to other students.

ORANGE – SPONTANEOUS SUGGESTIONS
- I thought of a different game.
- Can we make this more fun?
- Let's start now! -OR- When are we going to start?
- Let's time ourselves.

ORANGE – DECISIONS/CHOICES
- I could build a model.
- We could set up teams.
- Let me be the teacher. (Often with new strategies)
- Can we score this test now?

NOTES:

GREEN Strengths:

Analyzing	Problem Solving
Conceptualizing	Reasoning
Confidence	Researching
Designing	Technical know-how
Determination	Thinking
Developing	Objectivity
Diagnosing	Forecasting
Intellectualizing	Understanding Abstract
Inventing	Perpetual Learner
Mapping	Tenacity

Copyright 2006 by Mary Miscisin – All rights reserved
www.PositivelyMary.com
Used with permission.

GREEN Preferences in the Learning Environment

Included in a lesson I would like Conceptualization.

I enjoy a lesson more when it includes Challenges.

I need opportunities for discovering Insights.

In a lesson I prefer Alternative Applications.

I take in information through Strategies.

Lessons can be supported by Problem Solving.

I am an Analytical Learner.

I am frequently Curious.

I prefer Research Opportunities.

I want my lessons to be Independent.

In most lessons, I pursue Invention.

I strive for Competence.

GREEN – STUDENT BEHAVIOR SAMPLES

GREEN – LINGO
What is that for?
I still don't understand.
What do you mean by that?
Is this correct?

GREEN – BODY LANGUAGE
Frequently sits alone at the short end of a rectangular table when in a group.
Turns away from the group to read.
Sits alone when possible to work a puzzle or read.
Refuses to answer a question. Gives the silent treatment.

GREEN – SPONTANEOUS SUGGESTIONS
Where can I find more information? Where can I learn more about this?
Do we have to work with a partner?
This could be improved. I can do better than this.
I can do this myself. I don't need help.

GREEN – DECISIONS/CHOICES
I could look this up in an encyclopedia or on the Internet.
I need to know more before I decide what to do.
We did this yesterday.
Could you explain this idea?

NOTES:

GOLD Strengths:

Belonging	Accounting
Care-taking	Organizing
Establishing Protocol	Planning Ahead
Contributing	Securing
Coordinating	Supervising
Dispatching	Work First/Play Later
Family	Decision Making
Following Directions	Completion
Guarding	Efficiency
Handling Details	Realistic

Copyright 2006 by Mary Miscisin – All rights reserved
www.PositivelyMary.com
Used with permission.

GOLD Preferences in the Learning Environment

Included in a lesson I would like Organization.

I enjoy a lesson more when it includes Rules.

I need opportunities for following Guidelines.

In a lesson I prefer Procedures.

I take in information through Materials.

Lessons can be supported by Scripting.

I am a Common Sense Learner.

I am frequently Responsible.

I prefer Tutoring, Being Helpful to Others.

I want my lessons to be Structured (Graphic Organizers).

I appreciate Accuracy.

I strive for Dependability.

GOLD – STUDENT BEHAVIOR SAMPLES

GOLD – LINGO
You have to do this. It's a school rule.
Should we number our papers, now?
Can we get another star, if it is all correct?
We have to read the rules of the game, first.

GOLD – BODY LANGUAGE
The first person to respond when called.
Pushes in chairs to make the room look nice.
This student has a neat desk.
Waits patiently to take turns.
Arranges school supplies before starting an assignment.

GOLD – SPONTANEOUS SUGGESTIONS
May we have classroom jobs?
Will we be using this again?
Can everybody come on time next time?
Can we set a due date, so I know?

GOLD – DECISIONS/CHOICES
May we copy the directions, first?
If we make a chart, it makes more sense.
We could graph the details, so the results can be seen more clearly.
May we finish this project before we have to start that one?

NOTES:

BLUE Strengths:

Accepting	Listening
Acting as a catalyst	Mentoring
Communicating	Motivating
Cooperating	Optimism
Counseling	Recruiting
Creating	Speaking
Guiding	Supportiveness
Imagination	Teaching
Intuition	Tolerant
Leading	Training

Copyright 2006 by Mary Miscisin – All rights reserved
www.PositivelyMary.com
Used with permission.

BLUE Preferences in the Learning Environment

Included in a lesson I would like Interaction.

I enjoy a lesson more when it includes Discussion.

I need opportunities for maintaining Cooperation.

In a lesson I prefer Information to Synthesize.

I take in information through Collaboration.

Lessons can be supported by Role Playing.

I am an Imaginative Learner.

I am frequently Harmonious.

I prefer Peer Tutoring, Reciprocal Teaching.

I want my lessons to be Interactive.

In most lessons, I pursue Personal Growth.

I strive for Empathy.

BLUE – STUDENT BEHAVIOR SAMPLES

BLUE – LINGO
May we discuss this, first?
Am I doing this right?
Good try. Maybe you'll win next time?
Gee that looks nice. Good luck!

BLUE – BODY LANGUAGE
Turns to look at other students to listen to them.
Puts arm on shoulder of another student, group hugs.
Gives "High Fives" or other physical expressions of group success.
Talks with many hand gestures.

BLUE – SPONTANEOUS SUGGESTIONS
May we draw now?
I can think of a happier ending for this story.
May we use "make-believe" voices when we read?
May we perform a play together?

BLUE – DECISIONS/CHOICES
Chooses cooperative tasks when possible.
Helpful to another student or teacher.
Chooses essay assignments over "fill-in" worksheets or puzzles.
Passes out supplies to everyone, usually asks permission.

NOTES:

Solutions for Fractions for Applications

These fractions are more challenging and can be used for additional **4-COLOR LESSONS**.

The parts-to-whole relationships for the following fractions:

$\dfrac{5}{8}$ = 0.625 = 62.5%

$\dfrac{1}{3}$ = 0.3333 = 33%
1/3 is less than half so remainder is usually dropped.

$\dfrac{5}{6}$ = 0.83333 = 83%
1/3 is less than half so remainder is usually dropped.

$\dfrac{1}{6}$ = 0.1666 = 17%
1/6 is larger than half so remainder is usually rounded up.

$\dfrac{7}{9}$ = 0.7777 = 78%
7/9 is larger than half so remainder is usually rounded up.

$\dfrac{1}{7}$ = 0.1428571 = 14%
When 2 is the last digit = 14%
When 8 is the last digit = 14.3%
When 5 is the last digit = Either drop or round up.

*******   *******   *******   *******

As you gain more knowledge of **Color Styles** principles and integrate the principles in your lesson planning, you will enjoy implementing and experimenting with <u>**4-COLOR LESSONS**</u> using more of the preferences and strengths.

For more information about **Color Styles** go to this web site: www.PositivelyMary.com.

*******   *******   *******   *******

CPSIA information can be obtained at www.ICGtesting.com
Printed in the USA
LVIW01n0245031117
554857LV00001B/8